Nola The Nurse

Remembers Hurricane Katrina

Coloring Book

by Dr. Scharmaine L. Baker, NP.

illustrated by Marvin Alonso

A DrNurse
Publishing House

New Orleans, Louisiana

COPYRIGHT ©2015 by Dr. Scharmaine L. Baker and its licensors.
All rights reserved.

No part of this book may be reproduced or transmitted in any form or by any means, electronic or mechanical, including photocopy, recording, or by any information storage and retrieval system without the written permission of the publisher or author except where permitted by law.

For information address A DrNurse Publishing House
2475 Canal Street, Suite 240, new Orleans, La. 70119
www.NolatheNurse.com

ISBN-13: 978-0-692-59647-0
ISBN-10: 0-692-59647

Author Contact info:
info@DrBakerNP.com
@NolaTheNurse
@DrBakerNP
www.DrBakerNP.com
www.NolaTheNurse.com

Bax The Nurse

Charo The CRNA

Dr. Baker
Nurse Practitioner

Dr. Eden
Nurse Practitioner

Gumbo

About The Author...

Dr. Scharmaine L. Baker, NP is a nationally recognized and award-winning nurse practitioner in New Orleans, Louisiana. She has received numerous honors and awards for her contributions to healthcare in New Orleans since she became a family nurse practitioner in 2000, including the 2013 Healthcare Hero award (New Orleans City Business magazine) and 2008 Entrepreneur of the Year award (ADVANCE for Nurse Practitioner magazine).

Dr. Baker has a doctor of nursing practice (DNP) degree from Chatham University in Pittsburgh, PA, and she is a fellow of the American Association of Nurse Practitioners (AANP). She was inspired to make house calls while caring for her grandmother, who was ill and needed an in-home doctor.

After Hurricane Katrina, Dr. Baker was instrumental in caring for the sick and disabled in New Orleans, where hospitals had closed and doctors had evacuated but never returned. Her patient load went from 100 to 500 in only three months. Thanks to her passion and unwavering dedication to caring for homebound patients in her home town, Dr. Baker's story was featured on the CBS Evening News with Katie Couric.

Today, Dr. Baker maintains a busy private practice in New Orleans by making house calls to the elderly and disabled who would otherwise not receive healthcare.

When this award-winning and nationally known nurse practitioner is not on the road delivering keynote speeches and attending various other media events, she loves reading to her children, Skylar Rose and Wyatt Shane.

www.DrBakerNP.com
www.NolaTheNurse.com
http://shop.DrBakerNP.com

www.ingramcontent.com/pod-product-compliance
Lightning Source LLC
Chambersburg PA
CBHW082247300426
44110CB00039B/2465